Peter Peckard

Justice and Mercy Recommended, Particularly With Reference to the Slave Trade

A sermon preached before the University of Cambridge

Peter Peckard

Justice and Mercy Recommended, Particularly With Reference to the Slave Trade
A sermon preached before the University of Cambridge

ISBN/EAN: 9783337411077

Printed in Europe, USA, Canada, Australia, Japan

Cover: Foto ©Lupo / pixelio.de

More available books at **www.hansebooks.com**

Juſtice and Mercy recommended, particularly with reference to the SLAVE TRADE.

A

S E R M O N

PREACHED BEFORE THE

UNIVERSITY OF CAMBRIDGE,

By P. P E C K A R D, D.D.

MASTER OF MAGDALEN COLLEGE.

C A M B R I D G E,

Printed by J. ARCHDEACON Printer to the UNIVERSITY;

For J. & J. MERRILL, in Cambridge; T. CADELL, in the Strand; B. WHITE & Son, in Fleet-ſtreet; T. PAYNE & Son, at the Mews Gate; T. EVANS, in Paternoſter-Row; and G. & T. WILKIE, in St. Paul's Church Yard, London.

MDCCLXXXVIII.

TO THE RIGHT REVEREND

BEILBY,

LORD BISHOP OF LONDON.

WITHOUT permiſſion aſked, my Lord, and even without your knowledge to take this liberty, may perhaps be thought a great degree of preſumption. Poſſibly it may really be ſo. Yet to whom can I with ſo much propriety inſcribe the following humble recommendation of Juſtice and Mercy, as to him who hath nobly diſtinguiſhed himſelf in the ſame cauſe, and ſtood forth publickly the Patron of Benevolence and Humanity.

A 2

I look

I look back, my Lord, with fe-cret pleafure on paft times, and with great fatisfaction of mind recollect thofe happy hours of private inter-courfe which I have enjoyed with you in my fequeftered fituation. And I well remember that the fub-ject which I have weakly touched in the enfuing difcourfe, was not un-frequently a Topic of our converfa-fation. Our fentiments then agreed : I am happy to find they do fo ftill, and wifh from my foul that not only your Lordfhip, but that all the world agreed with me in receiving with horror the very idea of Slavery and Inhumanity.

I live in great meafure out of the world, and hear on but very flight authority what is going forward in it. There feems to be reafon to hope that a moft refpectable affocia-tion is now forming to effect, if poffi-

ble,

ble, the Abolition of the Slave Trade, that abominable violation of the Laws of God, and the common Rights of Man.

No difficulty of any confequence can attend the carrying it into execution, nor can any perfonal injury be pretended, if the TOTAL abolition be determined with refpect to FUTURE time, and a proper mode of gradual emancipation eftablifhed with refpect to thofe poor creatures who at prefent fuffer this enormous injuftice. I have feen a practicable fcheme drawn up by a very worthy member of your reverend bench, which would be effectual to this purpofe, and to which in my opinion there is not a rational objection. The Spaniards have in fome of their fettlements, as I am informed, carried a fimilar plan into execution, and find great benefit refulting from it. A

very

very refpectable Sect of our diffent-
ing brethren (on many accounts very
refpectable indeed, particularly in
their reverence for the majefty and
the name of God, in their difappro-
bation of war, and their fixed abhorrence of every fpecies of inhumanity) have in refpect of the Slave
Trade fet us a very amiable example.
May we have the virtue to follow it!

As to our movements at home upon this fubject, I hear mentioned the
honoured names of WILBERFORCE
and SHARP, as Leaders in this glorious
undertaking. Their known and eftablifhed virtues muft furely induce
many to join in this great work of
Juftice and Mercy: and may Heaven
profper and reward their Labours!

Your great city, my Lord, the firft
in eminence, ftands the foremoft in
this truly Chriftian Charity. The
towns of Manchefter and Birmingham,

ham, places of great importance, have already joined in following the good example, and giving their support. Other places are named, and it is to be hoped there will not be many either places or perfons in whom the mercenary gripe of felf-intereft will totally eradicate the generous emotions of Philanthropy.

We from this Univerfity fhew, by our Addrefs to the Legiflature, and by the Contribution of our Mite, that the precepts of moral inftruction have not been thrown away upon us; and no doubt our more opulent Academical Sifter will beftow her richer offerings, in order to bring forward with full effect the application to the Legiflature for the TOTAL ABOLITION OF THE SLAVE TRADE.

With refpect to myfelf, my fphere of action is very contracted indeed: and I now ftep forth, a volunteer,

with

with humility yet with refolution to offer rather my inclination than ability to ferve. My efforts, probably, can reach little farther than to infufe into the minds of the young men committed to my care, principles of reverence for our unrivaled Conftitution, of Loyalty to the King, the Patron and Example of Juftice and Mercy; of Obedience to Magiftrates, and of Univerfal Benevolence: and thus on the folid foundation of true Virtue eventually ferve the good Caufe, to which I moft devoutly wifh all poffible fuccefs.

When I was firft called to this place, I had conceived fome thoughts to attempt fomething upon this fubject, which was always near my heart; but being diffident of my own ftrength, and recollecting the fate of the poor man (James ii. 2.) when One with a gold ring and goodly apparel came into

the

the affembly, I defifted from my intentions. For thofe great perfonages are too apt, if the Poor man fpeak, to fay, What fellow is this? and if he ftumble they will help to overthrow him. (Ecclus. xiii. 23.)

When I had the honour, about three years fince, to ferve the principal office in this Univerfity, I gave the Indefenfiblenefs of Slavery as a fubjeƈt for the Public Exercifes of the Batchelors; and Mr. Clarkfon's performance which gained the Prize, has been laid before the world in more than one edition. Thus, through him, I look upon myfelf as in fome fmall degree a Promoter of the glorious attempt to fet the Slave at Liberty.

A century of years hath now paffed fince Providence beftowed upon us, on the fure ground of Conftitutional Eftablifhmcnt, the ineftimable bleffings of Liberty Civil and Rcligious.

Lct

Let this year then be a Jubilee of Commemoration: not in noify riot and drunkennefs, not in diforder and tumult, but by extending the blef-fings we enjoy to thofe who are de-prived of them; by breaking every yoke, and fetting the poor Captive free.

My motive, my Lord, for taking this liberty with you, muft be alfo my apology—an impulfe of Confcience to contribute my feeble endeavours, but principally an earneft defire to incite fome more able advocate—

—fungar vice cotis, acutum
Reddere quæ ferrum valet, exfors ipfe fecandi.

From every candid reader alfo I muft folicit his indulgence for the many inaccuracies—

——quas aut incuria fudit
Aut humana parum cavit natura—

But why then trouble the Public with Inaccuracies that require this
indul-

Indulgence? I anfwer, There are indeed many in this place infinitely better qualified than I am to do Juftice to the Subject, and with fincere pleafure I fhould have feen any of them undertake this benevolent office. But none ftood forth: it was wifhed that fome one would; and therefore I made an offer of my weak efforts in the enfuing difcourfe; which was at firft intended only for the private Chapel of a fmall Society, but now by an unexpected fate is humbly prefented to your Lordfhip's protection.

May you, my Lord, experience every earthly blefling! may you long enjoy in health and happinefs your honourable and exalted Station! and may your pious labours here be hereafter rewarded with never-ending felicity!

P. PECKARD.

Magdalen College,
Jan. 31, 1788.

SERMON, &c.

MICAH vi. 8.

HE HATH SHEWED THEE, O MAN, WHAT IS
GOOD, AND WHAT DOTH THE LORD RE-
QUIRE OF THEE BUT TO DO JUSTLY, TO
LOVE MERCY, AND TO WALK HUMBLY
WITH THY GOD.

THAT God is both able and willing
to direct man to his proper happinefs,
is evidently deducible from his acknowledged attributes of unlimited Power and
Goodnefs.

He who created us, and gave us all our faculties, is undoubtedly able to influence and
direct thofe faculties in what manner and to
what degree he himfelf fhall judge proper.

He whofe mercy is over all his works,
who knows whereof we are made, and that
with

without his affifting hand we fhould be loft in ignorance and mifery, undoubtedly will not withhold that affiftance which is proper for our fituation.

The known ftate of the world in the different periods and different circumftances of it's Exiftence, plainly prove that where the knowledge of a fuperintending Providence is by any means loft, there ignorance, and mifery prevail, and every bad paffion that can difgrace a rational being is predominant. On the contrary, where the fenfe of an overruling Providence hath been kept alive, and the duties naturally refulting from it properly attended to, there we find the feat of virtue and of happinefs.

Thefe are known truths that bring peace and comfort with them : and on this ground we may make the following equitable conclufion, That wherefoever men will keep God in their thoughts, and duly attend to the notices he is pleafed to beftow, he does at all times, and in all places fhew them what is for their Good.

In what way it may pleafe the Almighty to communicate to us thefe notices conducive to our happinefs, perhaps, in our prefent ftate, it may be impoffible for us fully

to

to conceive, and certainly would be a blameable curiofity to enquire. We ought to be thankful for the blefling, and not be over follicitous to know the precife means by which we receive it. Yet in general we may fay, I hope without prefumption,

Firft, That God hath fhewn us what is Good by the frame and conftituion of our nature, originally difpofed by him to receive in due time diftinct impreffions of Good and Evil, of Right and Wrong, with a Natural Tendency to be. pleafed with the one, and to féel an abhorrence of the other.

Secondly, That he hath at fundry times, and in diverfe manners, ftrengthened and affifted thefe original tendencies of our Nature by various communications of his revealed Will.

Firft then, if I may be allowed to fpeak, and to judge of a Moral Senfe of Good and Evil by analogy from the other fenfes with which God hath bleffed us, it is plain beyond all doubt, that there are fome objects that are naturally agreeable, others that are naturally difagreeable. All colours are not equally pleafant to the eye, all founds to the ear, all fcents to the faculty of fmelling, nor all taftes to the palate. Some are originally

ginally offenfive in a high degree, while others are in an equal degree delightful. And although thefe may, from fubfequent caufes, be greatly changed, infomuch that thofe things which were originally pleafant or difgufting, fhall at length have a contrary effect; yet this is not the work of Nature, but of Education, or other fubfequent and fecondary caufes. By degrees we are taught to diflike what was once agreeable, and to receive with pleafure what was originally offenfive.

So may it be with refpect to what I mean by a Moral fenfe of Good and Evil. I have not the leaft doubt, but that when the human conftitution is fo far advanced that Reafon begins to act, and judgments can be formed, and diftinct notions framed of Right and Wrong, the approbation of Good, and the diflike of Evil, will arife from the Original Conftitution of human nature.

I hope I fhall not be fo mifunderftood as to be thought to advance the doctrine of Innate Ideas, or Innate Inftincts. I mean no fuch thing. I fuppofe only, that as foon as the Faculty of Perception exifts, there will be a difference of Perceptions. That with refpect to Senfation from exter-

nal

nal objects, if a child at it's birth be feverely
fmitten with a rod, or lightly touched with
a feather, be expofed to extremity of pierc-
ing cold, or foftered by a genial warmth,
the perceptions will be very different, and
one will be attended with pleafure, the
other with pain.

In a manner fomething analogous to this,
when the mental perceptions take place, I
think that Impreffions of Virtue, Goodnefs,
Generofity, Benevolence, fuppofing the ab-
fence of Prejudice, will be infinitely more
agreeable to the unbiaffed mind than Impreffions of a contrary quality. In this fenfe
I firmly believe that fo far our kind Creator
hath, by the very frame and conftitution of
our nature, fhewn to man what is Good.

By which I do not mean any fenfible impulfe, or irrefiftible influence, but only
fuch a difpenfation of things, as in the ope-
ration and effect, fhall appear nothing more -
than a good difpofition guiding the conduct
of man by motives of Difcretion, Virtue and
Religion.

From this view of the Human Conftitution, it muft manifeftly appear, that at leaft
there is not any natural repugnance againft
impreffions of Benevolence and Philantho-

B   py :

py: that the Social Affections of Compaf-
fion and Love for our fellow creatures. are
as much a part of our Nature, as thofe of
a more felfifh fort, and much more fo than
thofe which are mixed with malignity towards others. So that in all acts of Cruelty
we feem to fin againft Nature as much as
againft the Commands of God.

But Education hath it's Effect much
fooner than is generally thought. It is fel-
dom what it ought to be, and is fometimes
fo pernicious, that at length the whole order
and original conftitution of nature is per-
verted. And thus by degrees it comes to
pafs that we fee men with deliberation of
mind, approve what is abominably Evil;
approve even of Cruelty, and the fight of
Human Mifery; with coolnefs, with apa-
thy and fraudful circumvention opprefs,
enflave and torture their fellow creatures.
But this can never be till all the Social Affections are effaced, the work of God deftroyed, and the Original Conftitution of
Human Nature overturned. Nor can any
argument be taken from thefe inftances to
lead us to conclude, that even to thefe perfons, thus dreadfully depraved, God did not
originally fhew what is Good.

Secondly,

Secondly, he hath aſſiſted theſe Original Tendencies from our Conſtitution by gracious Communications of his Revealed Will. Of theſe there are various ſorts and different degrees recorded in the Scripture, which at ſundry times and in diverſe manners were beſtowed according to the circumſtances of times, and the exigencies of mankind.

It is but very little that is recorded of the Providential directions given to our firſt parents, but it plainly appears that there was both a Permiſſion, and a Prohibition, in order to ſhew Adam what was for his Good. " Of every Tree in the Garden thou mayeſt freely eat, but of the Tree of the Knowledge of Good and Evil : Thou ſhalt not eat of it : for in the day that thou eateſt thereof, thou ſhalt ſurely die." Now although this be an obſcure paſſage, and learned men have differed greatly in the ſenſes they have put upon it, yet ſo far is very plain, that whatſoever the preciſe meaning of it may be, it undoubtedly proves a communication of the Divine Will to Adam for his Good. So alſo in the intercourſe with Cain it is ſaid, If thou doeſt well ſhalt thou not be accepted? and if thou doeſt not well, Sin lieth at the door. This ſhews us plain,

almoſt

almoſt as words can make it, that ſome information had been given him for his Good, and that his obedience or tranſgreſſion would meet with due puniſhment or reward. Thus in the very infancy of the world did God condeſcend to ſhew man what is Good, in ſtrengthening the original tendencies of Nature by Communications of the Divine Will. And throughout the ſucceeding ages, during the times of the Patriarchs, by the Inſtitution of the Jewiſh Religion, and by the Inſpiration of the Prophets, the ſame methods of Providence were purſued, and God never ceaſed to ſhew to Man what is Good. Theſe communications were varied indeed according to the circumſtances of the times, but in general they gradually became more and more clear, as they approached nearer to the diſpenſation of the Goſpel, that full, that perfect, that final diſplay of the Will of God for the Good of Man.

Let us now reaſon a little upon this ſtate of things. God is our Creator, our Father. It is agreeable to Truth, and the Fitneſs of things, as it is expreſſed, that a Father ſhould ſhew an indulgent care of his children, that he ſhould inſtruct their ignorance,

rance, that he fhould beftow on them the means of improvement, that he fhould lead them to their proper Good. This it appears that God hath done for his children, both from the frame of their Conftitution, and by direct as well as intermediate communications with them. What then is the refult of all this care and tendernefs? Is it beftowed upon us without expectation of any return on our part? doth not a fenfe of gratitude and duty inform us that this cannot be? There is then fome requifition from us. God hath fhewn thee, O man, what is Good, and in return, what doth the Lord require of thee, but to do Juftly, to love Mercy, and to walk humbly with thy God. Juftice, Mercy, and Humility are then the great Requifites, and the Outlines of our Duty.

That Juftice from Man to Man is an indifpenfible obligation needs not any formal proof, becaufe it is felf-evident, that if men were permitted, according to their fuppofed neceffities, or their vicious inclinations, to be unjuft towards each other, nothing but univerfal difcord, confufion, and mifery muft be the immediate confequence. That this is an unqueftionable Truth, ap-

pears

pears too plainly from the miserable condition of those unhappy men oppressed with the Yoke of Slavery, in whose severe fate, inattention to the maxims of common justice produces universally the most insupportable state of human wretchedness. But farther, he who is unjust is a Thief and a Robber, because, so far as his injustice extends, he takes by fraud or violence that which belongs to another, and deprives him of his proper right. Now Society consists in the union of it's members and in every one's enjoying peaceably what is his own. But Injustice breaks this Union, and all peaceable enjoyments of Personal Property, and tends to the dissolution of Human Society. Justice therefore is enjoined us, in the first place as an absolute and indispensible duty, because men were formed to live in Society, and because Society cannot subsist but by a reciprocal observation of Justice.

There is not, it may be observed, any virtue in Justice, nor the least shadow of reward due to the practise of it: every one has a strict and absolute right to it from every other person. And we might as well pretend to merit for not putting out the eyes

eyes of our neighbour, or not depriving
him of his life, as to any virtue in refraining from Injuftice towards him. By the
practice of Juftice we only avoid being criminal. We are not in any degree profita-
ble fervants, we fhall have barely done
what it was our ftrict duty to do. When
therefore we hear fuch mighty praifes on
the character of the Honeft man, the word
Honefty muft be taken in fome extended
fignification, becaufe every one is under an
indifpenfible obligation to Honefty and
Juftice. Such praifes then are in truth
little better than cenfure on the practice of
the world, if thefe commendations are given
to the meer refraining from a Crime.

But our duty doth not reft here. We are in
the next place to love Mercy. There is a peculiar energy in this form of expreffion. We
are to do Juftly, but we are to love Mercy.
Let us then examine our real fituation with
refpect to this moft amiable of all human
virtues. And, firft, as it may be connect-
ed with Juftice in the redrefs of Injuries, or
the Punifhment of Offences.

In the adminiftration of Juftice for the
redrefs of Injuries we ought, no doubt, to
fee that compenfation be made to the in-

B 4   jured,

jured, but this fhould always be done without paffion, without malevolence, without
any unneceffary rigour. And fo far every
one has a right that Mercy fhould be mixed
with Juftice in the redrefs of Injuries.

In the adminiftration of Juftice for the
Punifhment of Offences, Mercy feems to
have a ftronger call upon us than in the redrefs of Injuries. In many things we all
offend; we fhould therefore have a fellow-
feeling for Offenders, and a confcioufnefs of
human weaknefs fhould teach us this com-
paffion as far as is confiftent with public
welfare. Doubtlefs there are fome crimes
of a nature fo atrocious as not to leave
room for Mercy—where punifhment muft
be for Example and for Terror: but in general, it is to be wifhed that our Penal Laws
were more equitably proportionate to offences, and more than they are at prefent
found, foftened by Mercy: more gentle in
the Penal Sentence, and in Execution more
determined.

But there is yet a far more extenfive field
open to us for the exertion of Mercy, than
the redrefs of Injuries, or the Punifhment
of Offences. Every creature that God hath
made, and endued with life and fenfibility,

is

is entitled to our Mercy. The moft perfect of human beings hath fome imperfec-
tions which may claim our pity; nor is the
humble worm which we tread under foot
beneath out tender regard. And yet, if we
take a difpaffionate view of our general conduct, with what horrror muft we contemplate our deviation from this godlike direction
to Love Mercy. Even the procurement of
our food, nay our very amufements are too
often founded in cruelty. What fhall we
fay to the general treatment of thofe Ani-
malts, which, though for our benefit placed
by Providence in a ftate of fubordination to
ourfelves, are yet endued with noble powers
and faculties both of Body and Mind? who
poffefs in high degree the fenfe of Pain and
Pleafure—who are confcious, as we ourfelves can be, of kind, and of cruel ufage
—who give evident proofs of Gratitude and
Affection. It fhould be for ever kept in
mind by us, That the righteous man is
merciful to his Beaft—but in this refpect
we have neither righteoufnefs nor mercy.
Yet they have all the fame common father
with ourfelves, the fame God created them.
" Who gave the horfe his ftrength, and
cloathed his neck with thunder? who
made

made the glory of his noftrils terrible? who taught him to paw in the valley, to mock at fear, and not to turn back from the fword?" and was he formed by an Almighty hand with thefe diftinctions, and was it given him to poffefs thefe fuperior qualities, and yet be doomed to the cruel fate which every where attends him? But this is a crime which muft hereafter be accounted for— God, in his benediction to Noah, hath declared, that for the blood, that is, for the cruel treatment of every inferior Animal he will require an account, " at the hand of every beaft will I require it."

Happy for us would it be did our Cruelty ftop here; happy, was it not extended to fuch a degree, and perpetrated with fuch horrid circumftances of favage ferocity, as feem to preclude all poffibility of pardon. When thoufands and ten times tens of thoufands of Innocent Men, through vile and mercenary motives are annually doomed to Slaughter, nay, to a ftate far worfe than than Slaughter, by premeditated contrivance, and infernal deliberation of mind. I have not in view the ravages of war; thefe are innocent paftimes compared with the fcenes of Cruelty to which I allude. I

mean

mean our eſtabliſhed, and to our eternal
ſhame be it ſaid, our Legal Traffick in Human Blood. In this view the thought is
beyond meaſure horrible: for while the
Legiſlature gives formal Sanction to this
Enormity, they make themſelves partakers,
and ſo involve the Nation in the dreadful
guilt of the Individuals immediately con-
cerned in theſe deeds of Oppreſſion, Cruelty, Murther.

We read of a Pharaoh, of a Nero, of
ſanguinary tyrants in the Eaſt: we read of
Kings nearer home, and nearer our own times
whoſe characteriſtic appellations were the
Cruel, the *Bloody*: yet we no where read of
any Character that for total want of Humanity ſtands equal to the Britiſh Merchant
in Men. In the former inſtances the
crimes indeed were great, but they were
the crimes of Individuals, giving an uncon-
trouled dominion to their vicious paſſions:
in the latter, the Evil is a Syſtematic Inſtitution of hardneſs of heart, and unexam-
pled barbarity. A ſpecies of merchandiſe
it is, founded in principles that ſtand in
direct oppoſition and in open defiance to
the peculiar and diſtinguiſhing commands
of our Saviour; and this too in the face of
the

the world, patronized by the Legiflature of
a Nation, profeffing itfelf Chriftian. Afto-
nifhing Contradiction! I do not mean to
infinuate, that the Chriftian Inftitution in
exprefs terms prohibits Slavery.; it fuppofes
fuch a Practice to have fubfifted.; yet the
directions given to perfons in a ftate of Ser-
vitude are not to be confidered as an approbation of that practice, but merely from it's
fpirit of accommodation, and to preferve
peace both in families and ftates, as a rule
of obedient conduct to thofe who were in
that unhappy fituation. For the Spirit of
Chriftianity abhors the very idea; teaches
us that with God there is no fuch refpect of
Perfons, and that in his fight the poor
flave, who patiently fuffers, is of greater
merit than the Tyrant who inflicts his fuf-
ferings.

An Enormity this of fuch magnitude,
that with the circumftances preceding the
very act, the act itfelf, and the certain
known confequences attending it, the An-
nals of the whole world cannot produce it's
equal in perfidy, injuftice, and cruelty : being radically, abfolutely, and effentially
Evil, loaded with all poffible malignity,
and totally deftitute of any Real Good. It
is

is therefore not juftifiable by the Sanction of any Human Inftitution. For not even Political Neceffity can be juftly pleaded for it, which, fome men feem to think, can change the very Effence of Actions.

A refpectable writer upon Morals, in the diftinction between Things and Perfons, obferves, that Man being a Perfon cannot make himfelf a Thing, fo as to become the Property of another Man. This obfervation may be corroborated by reflecting, that every Man immediately upon his birth, and throughout the whole courfe of his life, is already a Property belonging to a fuperior Lord, and therefore cannot make himfelf the Property of an inferior. He is for ever the Property of God. " It is God who hath made us, and not we ourfelves; we are HIS people, and the Sheep of HIS pafture." Nor can we, without Guilt, alienate this Property of God, or transfer it from him to Man. We have not any authority fo to do, for we belong to God. Hence we cannot difpofe of our own Life or commit Suicide without being Criminal. On the fame reafoning that We ourfelves, and all that is generally called Our Own, belongs ftrictly to God, appears the propriety

priety of a future day of Refponfibility,
when for all our Actions done in the Body,
and for the Ufe or Abufe of all our Talents
and Faculties we muft render an Account
to God. All which Talents and Faculties are
therefore called by our Saviour, That which
is *Another's* [a], as being not independently
our Own Property, but only of that fort of
Poffeffion which is in the Nature of a Truft,
and over which Another, that is, God, hath
the Superior and Sovereign claim. No
man, therefore, can affign abfolutely over
to another Himfelf, and all his Powers and
Faculties, which is only a Poffeffion of
Truft from God without robbing God of
his Right. But every man who makes
himfelf a Slave is guilty of this Robbery.
And if no one has a right to do this himfelf, undoubtedly no other can do it for
him. This feems to imply that Slavery is
originally, and fundamentally indefenfible,
being effentially Evil: but our Mode of
carrying on this bufinefs, the point I have
particularly in view, is the deliberate per-
petration of a Crime againft God under all
the moft horrid circumftances of cruel

[a] Luke xvi. 12. το αλλοτριον.

aggra-

aggravation : it is therefore a tranfgreffion of the command, To Love Mercy.

Some idle pleas have been made for it from long cuftom, and the practice of the world : but this way we might juftify every vice of man. Some excufe has been offered from a pretended inferiority in the confti-tution of thefe unfortunate men : that they are untractable, and muft be ruled with a rod of Iron. This is what every Tyrant can fay in defence of his Tyranny. And were it true in this inftance, is it to be *it* wondered at, or is it to be condemned, if men are untractable, who, by fraud and violence, have not only been deprived of every endearment of Life, but are continu-ally torn by the ftings and lafhes of their unfeeling tormentors. It has alfo been pretended that they are of lower intellectual abilities than the reft of mankind. Suppofe it were fo, does this give us a right to enflave and torment them? But this is abfolutely falfe : God made of one blood all the fons of men : and many inftances have appeared to prove, that with refpect to Mental Pow-ers, they want only equal information to equal the inhabitants of the more enlight-
ened

ened Nations of the Earth [b]. In refpect of Gratitude, inviolable Affection, and every amiable quality of mind, where they have been humanely treated, they ftand in an unrivaled Superiority. Some have attempted, in a general way, to juftify Slavery from Captivity, from Infolvency, on account of Crimes, or from the Defpotifm in the State, but whatfoever weight thefe reafons may have in cafes where they can be admitted, yet here they lofe all their force, and are totally inapplicable to this vile traffick of the Britifh Man-Merchant. For with refpect to this nefarious commerce they are not founded in truth, and if they were true they are not defenfible [c]. But all

the

---

[b] See the Letters of Ignatius Sancho, and the Poems by Phyllis.

[c] Amongft various equally unjuft and cruel methods of fupplying our Ships with Slaves, the Prince of the Country, if he is not provided with fufficient numbers, will fometimes furround a village full of innocent and peaceable inhabitants with his troops: and fetting fire to the place, the unfortunate creatures thus circumvented, muft either perifh in the flames, or fall into his hands. The latter are fold to our Men-Merchants, who fell thofe they do not deftroy in the voyage to the Planters: who in their cruelty are thus far kind, that it is exerted to fuch degree as to be intolerable by the human frame, and therefore but few of thefe unfortunate creatures live many years. In thefe inftances, neither Captivity, properly fpeaking, nor Infolvency, nor Crimes can poffibly

the fhallow arguments that have been produced from thefe and fimilar Topics, as
Palliations of Injuftice and Juftifications of
Cruelty, are founded in falfehood and de-
ception; and it appears, on fair examina-
tion, that this commerce militates againft
worldly profit as much as againft common
Humanity. So that the purchafers of Men
from the Men-ftealers, feem to be under a
judicial infatuation, while they clearly act
againft their own temporal, as well as their
eternal intereft in the unparallelled barba-
rities which they daily, and hourly, and
every moment inflict upon their poor tortured fellow creatures; fince even their mercenary views would be better anfwered if
they could pay the leaft attention to the
calls, the duties of Humanity. For the
intolerable hardfhips to which thefe unhappy men are generally fubjected, drive many

to

possibly be urged as a Juftification of the Practice. Defpotifm indeed is feen in it's true Colours, and whoever has
the effrontery to make ufe of fuch a plea, may he be feized
in fome fimilar way, and meet with fimilar treatment. For
it is a precept both in heathen and in Chriftian Ethics, that
as he would do to others he fhould be done unto himfelf.

It is calculated that by thefe inhuman practifes a hundred
thoufand people are annually murthered; and that fince the
commencement of the Traffick, nine millions of human
creatures have been deftroyed. *Ninety hundred thoufand.*
See the Summary View.

to Suicide from defpair, and many perifh from the confequences of a very juftifiable refiftance to the feverities of their unfeeling tafk mafters. While on the contrary, in the few inftances where they are well treated, they are found not to decreafe, but to multiply [d], to retain their vigour, and perform their appointed labours with refignation to their hard Fate. From fuch Abfurdity of Conduct in their hard-hearted tyrants, one might imagine that fome malignant Demon firft infatuates them and then deftroys [e].

That the Legiflature of a Nation illuminated to a high degree by Science, human and divine, proud of Liberty Civil, Political and Religious, well acquainted with the Rights of Humanity, and pretending to the ftrict obfervance, not lefs than the knowledge of them, boafting every where of it's Charity and Benevolence, and encouraging Inftitutions for the relief of Human Mifery, that this Legiflature fhould yet give protection

---

[d] Seven plantations have wanted no fupplies for fome years. On thefe plantations the Negroes were treated with humanity. On one of them, where the treatment was fuperior to that of the reft, the numbers increafed fo much that the plantation was overftocked.

Summary View of the Slave Trade, p. 14.

[e] Quos vult perdere dementat prius.

protection to fuch wicked men in fuch wicked practices, is indeed an event which muft excite our aftonifhment, for which we muft pour forth the deepeft lamentation, of which we cannot think without horror, cannot fpeak but with indignation; and in this inftance certainly we may be angry, and fin not, even though the fun fhould go down upon wrath. But fhall not God vifit for fuch things, and fhall not his foul be avenged on fuch a Nation as this? Poffibly our Punifhment, if we repent not of thefe Evil doings, may not be far off : poffibly a ftate of worldly profperity may be the prelude to it : for when Individuals or Nations are become completely wicked,

—they are raifed aloft—
To make their fall more dreadful—[f]

Let us, however, hope that it is not yet too late to return to God. We are affured that when the Wicked turneth away from his wickednefs, and doeth that which is right, he fhall fave his Soul alive. We have formerly had Laws in this Country concerning Commutation for Murther, Laws concerning Witch-

---

[f] ——tolluntur in altum —
Ut lapfu graviore ruant—   Claud.

Witchcraft, Laws condemning to a cruel death for a difference in religious opinion. Thefe Laws for their Injuftice have been repealed. We have now Laws fubfifting concerning the Traffick in Human Blood[e]. Thefe Laws are equally unjuft, and may they foon have an equal fate, and may the Britifh Legiflature in this inftance, be entitled to honour for a due attention to the common rights of Humanity, the demands of Juftice, the cries of Mercy.

But it has been urged, that by virtue of thefe Laws, the public faith is pledged to thefe dealers in men for protection in the prefent mode of carrying on their bufinefs. So much the worfe: for neither the Public protecting, nor the Individuals protected have any right to pledge, or expect Faith for the Commiffion of Moral Evil; *for God hath*

---

[e] 5 Geo. 3. And be it farther enacted by the authority aforefaid, That it fhall not be lawful for any of the *Officers* or *Servants* employed by the Committee of the faid Company on the Coaft of Africa, to *export Negroes* from Africa upon *their own* Account—and if any fuch officer or fervant fhall be found, &c. he fhall be difmiffed, &c.

This claufe is written with a pen dipped in the heart's blood of thefe devoted Victims, thus delivered by the Legiflature of Britain to be EXPORTED as Goods of common merchandife by this African Committee: for whofe greater Gain their fervants are prohibited from interference in this murtherous injuftice. This Bloody Statute is the Legiflative Act of Britifh Chriftians!

hath not given any man Licence to Sin. Eccl.
xv. 20.

Farther, in defence of the Purchafers· of
Men from the Men-ftealers, it has alfo been
faid, That we muft not do Evil that Good may'
come; and therefore we muft not do an inju‑
ry to thefe perfons in order either to fet their
Slaves at Liberty, or prevent a future pur‑
chafe. Let us join iffue upon this argument.
The pretended injury in this cafe is at the
worft, merely an inconvenience which may
foon and eafily be remedied: it has not any
thing in it of the nature of Moral Evil, and
will be in the higheft degree productive of
Moral Good. Whatfoever it may be, it arifes
originally from circumftances effentially and
morally Evil: therefore even to occafion this
inconvenience, is not doing, but removing
Evil that Good may come. A fkilful Surgeon
frequently occafions an inconvenience to
produce a greater Good: he muft go to the
bottom of the wound to promote a permanent
cure. But this argument may be retorted.
We muft not do Evil, it is faid, that Good
may come. Certainly therefore we muft not
be guilty of Perfidy, Cruelty, and Murther,
the higheft inftances of moral Evil, merely
that the Planter may with the greater eafe

cultivate

cultivate his Plantation. And if this be true, which cannot be denied, there never would be any flaves to be tortured, or fet at Liberty.

But it is farther faid, that you cannot devife any mode of proceeding preferable to the prefent, fince it is the real Intereft of the Planter to fee that his flaves are treated with gentlenefs and humanity. Intereft is doubtlefs a powerful motive: but alas! do we not every day fee many inftances in which men deliberately act in direct contradiction to their true intereft? It is the true intereft of every one to be temperate, virtuous, prudent. Are there then none who are intemperate, vitious, imprudent? How many are there born to affluence and independance, who never are at reft till they have made themfelves wretched, defpicable dependants! Their real intereft has no weight with them when a fcandalous paffion is to be gratified, neither has it with the Dealer in Men.

Far

<hr />

f On one plantation in Barbadoes, by the cruelty of the Planter, in two years the number of his flaves was reduced from 170 to 95 : and at his death it was found that his inhuman feverity had not encreafed his Fortune. While on another plantation on the fame ifland, though in a lefs favourable fituation, by the humane and gentle treatment of the Mafter, who was as a father to his Negroes, they multiplied to a great degree. He purchafed a fecond eftate, and at his death, with the higheft character for his tendernefs and humanity, he had more than doubled his original fortune.

Far be it from me to wish the least detriment to these persons: I most devoutly wish their Reformation, and their true happiness; and mean only to insinuate that the argument from wordly interest hath not any conclusive weight as operating effectually upon the Planter's mind; or if it had, that the end proposed would be better answered by the employment of Persons in a state of Civil Liberty.

There are doubtless different ways of considering this subject, as Politicians, and as Christians. The Politician considers things of this nature merely as subjects of Political Casuistry without any regard to Moral Rectitude: the Christian looks to a more important end, which is not attainable but by a conduct that is Holy, Just, and Good. The Evils which the Politician fears or pretends to fear, are Imaginary: the Evils which the Christian actually sees, are Real, are Horrible; are of a Maglignity for which there cannot be any compensation by any worldly advantage whatsoever.

Let us then treat this matter as true and tenderhearted Christians. Let us look with an eye of Pity upon those who are fast bound in misery and iron: let us consider those who are thus bound as being bound with them:

let

let us break their bonds afunder, and caft away their cords from us: let us give light and liberty to thofe who fit in darknefs, and the fhadow of Death, and from a ftate of mifery and torture, let us guide their feet into the Paths of Peace.

Why the Almighty hath not fhewn the lighting down of his arm, and inftantaneoufly blafted the offenders by fome fevere ftroke of his indignation — why thefe enormities have hitherto been permitted, we cannot prefume to fay: we muft not too curioufly pry into the fecret difpenfations of Providence—thefe are amongft the things that require us to walk humbly with our God.

In truth, there are myfterious things in all the works and all the ways of God, that fhew the propriety of the concluding precept in the Text. But as we are certain that his difpenfations are all derived from infinite Goodnefs and Mercy, our duty is Refignation to his Will, and a refolution to walk Humbly with our God, till that time fhall come when this myfterious veil fhall be drawn afide, and every thing be made known unto us as clearly as we ourfelves are known to him who made us.

In this refigned and humble ftate of mind, we

we may without murmuring contemplate thofe circumftances which elfe muft hurt every one endued with fenfibility and benevolence, while they exhibit the great Theatre of Nature, whether in the Air, or on the Earth, or in the Waters under the Earth, as a Scene of Violence and Depredation. Far different this from that promifed ftate of things, when the Earth fhould be full of the Mercy of the Lord, and peace and happinefs eftablifhed throughout his holy Mountain.

In this ftate of mind, we may with lefs difcompofure contemplate even thofe horrible deeds already faintly fketched, and reft in hope that God in his good time will foften the flinty hearts of our Men-ftealers, and Men-purchafers, and touch them with a fpark of Mercy.

In this ftate of mind, we may with refignation contemplate that apparently unequal diftribution of things in the worldly profperity of wicked men, and in the depreffion and diftrefs of thofe who are of modeft Merit and unaffuming Virtue.

In this ftate of mind, we may with chearful fubmiffion contemplate our own origin from the Duft of the Earth, and our approaching

proaching refolution into the fame ftate of
Original Infenfibility, under the Firm belief and expectation, that God in his appointed feafon, will a fecond time beftow
upon us not only Senfibility, but Immortali-
ty. A revolution this in the circumftances
of Man's Exiftence which utterly confounds
all Human Philofophy that doth not admit
the Truth, and the Mediatorial Efficacy of
the Chriftian Difpenfation, by which alone
we gain a rational and authoritative affurance
of *The Refurrection and the Life*.

In this ftate of mind, we may without re-
pining, contemplate the Origin and Progrefs
of thofe Corruptions, which by fubftituting
the traditions of men in place of the Commands of God, have in feveral inftances
efpecially under the Papal Hierarchy made
the word of God of none effect: under the
fpecious term of Orthodoxy defacing the
genuine fimplicity of the Gofpel, and by the
introduction and intermixture of Opinions
and Doctrines, from the Schools of Heathen
Philofophy, laying foundation for the peculiar Errors of Popery. With equal refignation alfo, on the contrary, we may contemplate thofe parts of the Divine Difpenfations that ftill remain really myfterious,
and

and which, from imperfect views, have sometimes led hasty reasoners into Infidelity. While on one hand, seeing some things admitted into Systems of Christianity that appear to them evidently false, they precipitately conclude that nothing there is true; or on the other, presuming that the Human Understanding is commensurate to every object of it's investigation, they reject every thing that to them has the least appearance of Mystery. But these are extremes that are very blameable. For though additions or corruptions may obscure, they do not annihilate Truth; and though many things manifestly appear, and are easily known, yet there are still many things concealed, which in our present state of imperfect and confined faculties, we shall never know, and which for the present are proper objects of our Faith, and proper proofs of our Humility. For now we see but through a glass darkly, but the time will soon come when we shall see face to face.

When that awful period shall arrive, our Humility shall receive it's reward, and these mysterious parts of the Divine Dispensations be made clear and manifest to us as the Sun when he goeth forth in his might.

In

In the mean time let us, with abfolute refignation of Soul, and with the deepeft gratitude receive what God hath hitherto
fhewn us for our Good; let us with unre-
mitted perfeverance continue To do Juftly,
to love Mercy, and to walk humbly with
our God.

LONDON, 15th Jan. 1788.

At a Committee of the Society, inftituted for the Purpofe of effecting the ABOLI- TION of the SLAVE TRADE.

RESOLVED, That the following Report be circulated for the general Information of the Society.

THIS Committee would gladly have availed them- felves of the fentiments and inftructions of a Ge- neral Meeting of the Society, in profecuting the impor- tant objects of their appointment, but the remote fitua- tion of moft of the fubfcribers, creates a difficulty which cannot eafily be obviated. The Committee, however, beg leave to affure them, that due attention will be paid to fuch communications as they may be favoured with from individual members, and which it feems impracti- cable to obtain from the collective body.

The information and arguments on this fubject, con- tained in various publications, have fully evinced the injuftice and inhumanity of the Slave Trade. The Committee have expended a confiderable fum in print- ing and difperfing fuch tracts; but as they are fully per- fuaded, that no further arguments are neceffary on that head, they have more particularly directed their attention to the plea of political neceffity, which is frequently urg- ed to juftify, or at leaft to palliate, this traffick. For though it can by no means be admitted, that the greateft commercial advantages ought to preponderate, when oppofed to the plaineft dictates of religion and morality, yet the Committee are not infenfible of the natural in- fluence which intereft has in biaffing the judgements of

men

men, and of how much importance it is to convince the publick, that the commerce of this kingdom, and even the interest of the Slave-Holders themselves, will be advanced by the success of our endeavours.

With this view the Committee have been, and still are, engaged, at no inconsiderable expence, in promoting inquiries into the nature and conduct of the Slave Trade. These inquiries have not only produced fresh instances of the cruelties perpetrated on the wretched natives of Africa, but have established a fact, hitherto but little known, namely, the destruction of our seamen; for it appears that the lives of a very considerable proportion of those engaged in this trade, are annually sacrificed to the nature of the service, and the extreme severity of their treatment. To the abilities and unremitting assiduity of the Rev. Mr. Thomas Clarkson, in these researches, the Society are much indebted.

It must be acknowledged, that the amount of British manufactures exported to the coasts of Africa, for the purposes of this commerce, is considerable; but there is room to apprehend, that the demand for these would be much greater, if, in the place of it, was substituted an amicable intercourse, which, instead of spreading distress and devastation amongst the unoffending inhabitants, would introduce the blessings of peace and civilization. The Committee find, that several vessels have, for some time, been solely employed in the importation of many valuable productions of that country, of essential advantage to the manufactures of this: and they are in possession of sundry specimens of its produce, which confirm their belief, that the confidence of the natives being once established, a trade may be opened with them, which, without interfering with the principal staple commodities of our West-India Colonies, would speedily become of great national importance.

The Committee have several well authenticated accounts of estates in the West-Indies, on which the number of negroes has been not only supported, but increased, without any foreign supply for many years: a circumstance which affords the strongest proof that the nature of the case will admit, that a proper attention to the principles

ciples of humanity in their treatment would preclude the neceffity of any further fupplies from the coafts of Africa.

The Committee feel it their duty to diffufe the information they have obtained as generally as poffible, and more particularly to avail themfelves of every opportunity (in which they earneftly requeft the affiftance of every individual) of impreffing on the minds of our legiflators, the neceffity of entering into a ferious inveftigation of the fubject; and they have great fatisfaction in reporting that many very refpectable Members of both Houfes of Parliament have affured them of their difpofition to promote our defign.

The applications of the Committee have generally met with a cordial reception, and indeed perfons of refpectable fituation in many parts of the kingdom have afforded unfolicited fupport. Several men of learning have efpoufed the caufe in various publications. The Clergy of the eftablifhed Church, and the Minifters amongft the Diffenters, there is good reafon to believe are in general fincere friends to the undertaking. Members of both Univerfities have expreffed themfelves in terms of approbation of the plan; and, together with thefe, the fpirited exertions of Manchefter, Birmingham, and other principal Manufacturing Towns, afford ground to hope that a fpecies of oppreffion, fo difgraceful to the nation, will at length be abolifhed by general confent. And they truft, that whatever difficulties may attend their progrefs, by a fteady perfeverance the Society will eventually be inftrumental to the fuccefs of a caufe, in which are involved the honour of this country, and the happinefs of millions of our fellow-creatures.

During the attention of the Committee to the bufinefs, undoubted accounts have been received from North America, of the good conduct and capacity of many of the negroes refident there, with fpecimens of their improvement in ufeful learning, at a fchool eftablifhed in Philadelphia for their education, which fatisfactorily prove the abfurdity of the notion, that their underftandings are not equally fufceptible of cultivation with thofe of white people.

The Committee have likewife received information
from

from France, that there is a probability of a Society being eftablifhed there on the fame principles as our own.

The prefent amount of Subfcriptions received is
£. 1367. 8 s. 2 d.; and of our Payments already made,
£. 514. 17 s. 10 d. Though it is forefeen that the future expences in this bufinefs will be confiderable, it is
impoffible to afcertain the amount; but the liberal con-
tributions now reported, leave no room to doubt that
fuch further affiftance will be cheerfully given as will be
requifite to complete the purpofes of the inftitution.
The Committee truft it is unneceffary to add, that to thefe
purpofes only they fhall be faithfully applied.

Signed, by order of the Committee,

GRANVILLE SHARP, Chairman.